SQUADRONS!

No. 41

THE BRISTOL
BRIGAND

PHIL H. LISTEMANN

ISBN: 979-1096490-66-0

GLOSSARY OF TERMS

PERSONEL :
(AUS)/RAF: Australian serving in the RAF
(BEL)/RAF: Belgian serving in the RAF
(CAN)/RAF: Canadian serving in the RAF
(CZ)/RAF: Czechoslovak serving in the RAF
(NFL)/RAF: Newfoundlander serving in the RAF
(NL)/RAF: Dutch serving in the RAF
(NZ)/RAF: New Zealander serving in the RAF
(POL)/RAF: Pole serving in the RAF
(RHO)/RAF: Rhodesian serving in the RAF
(SA)/RAF: South African serving in the RAF
(US)/RAF - RCAF : American serving in the RAF or RCAF

RANKS
G/C : Group Captain
W/C : Wing Commander
S/L : Squadron Leader
F/L : Flight Lieutenant
F/O : Flying Officer
P/O : Pilot Officer
W/O : Warrant Officer
F/Sgt : Flight Sergeant
Sgt : Sergeant
Cpl : Corporal
LAC : Leading Aircraftman

OTHER
ATA: Air Transport Auxiliary
CO : Commander
DFC : Distinguished Flying Cross
DFM : Distinguished Flying Medal
DSO : Distinguished Service Order
Eva. : Evaded
ORB : Operational Record Book
OTU : Operational Training Unit
PoW : Prisoner of War
PAF: Polish Air Force
RAF : Royal Air Force
RAAF : Royal Australian Air Force
RCAF : Royal Canadian Air Force
RNZAF : Royal New Zealand Air Force
SAAF : South African Air Force
s/d: Shot down
Sqn : Squadron
† : Killed

THE BRITSOL BRIGAND

By 1942 the RAF was looking for a replacement for the Bristol Beaufighter. Its success as a strike aircraft set the pattern for its successor – twin-engine, heavily armed etc. Therefore, Bristol offered two alternatives; a Beaufighter derivative or a Buckingham derivative (see p34). The option chosen was a redesigned Beaufighter with a new fuselage and the ambitious specification to fulfill three roles: long-range day fighter, high-speed torpedo attack aircraft, and dive bomber. Bristol worked on the project and, in March 1943, suggested its Type 164. Permission to proceed was given the following month, using the denomination 'Brigand TF Mk.I', along with approval for four prototypes (serials **MX988**, **MX991**, **MX994** and **MX997**). The latter would be cancelled, but was re-instated as **TX374**. The first flight took place on 4 December 1944 (MX988). The prototype was powered by two 2400 horsepower Bristol Centaurus VII engines. Trials were carried out over the following months and, apart from some issues readily fixed, the Brigand was considered a good aircraft. Therefore, the first order placed for 200 aircraft (**RH742-RH777**, **RH792-RH879**, **RH891-RH939** and **RH955-RH998**) was confirmed and production launched. However, the first aircraft arrived too late to see any action in Europe or in the Far East and, with VJ-Day, the order was reduced and the last 120 airframes cancelled. The first eleven production aircraft were delivered as torpedo-fighters, as designed initially, and used for service trials with Coastal Command with the intention of equipping Nos. 36 and 42 Squadrons. This never happened, though, as the Brigand's role changed when Air Staff conceded the concept of a coastal strike aircraft was now obsolescent. The aircraft already built, but not delivered, were converted to light bombers and became Brigand B.1s. The Brigand B.1 retained the four cannon armament, but the rear gun was removed. The cockpit enclosure was redesigned as a one-piece moulded transparency, giving an improved view and allowing for the hood to be rapidly jettisoned. Armour plate was retained and external bomb racks and rocket rails were fitted. This new role led to a second order for 52 Brigand B.1s (**VS812-VS839**, **VS854-VS877**). This order was not fully delivered as the last eight aircraft were cancelled and sixteen of them (**VS817-VS832**) were delivered as Met.3s (RH763 serving as a prototype), an unarmed meteorological reconnaissance version (the Brigand II, a training version of the Brigand, was never built). Deliveries took place between January 1946 and December 1949, with two 2500hp Bristol Centaurus 57 radial engines, but two more Brigand B.1s were built (**WB228** and **WB236**) and delivered in February 1951 to replace two examples sent to the Pakistan Air Force for evaluation (RH820 and RH821 as N1125 and N1126). Only one of those returned to the UK (to become **WA560** after overhaul). In all, 99 Brigand B.1s were built and 98 taken on RAF charge. This version, and the Met.3, would see service in operational RAF units.

In the meantime a late variant of the Brigand appeared in 1950, the Brigand T.4, an airborne interception radar training variant. This version was unarmed and was developed to train fighter navigators for night flying, which required having the student's rear cockpit blacked out. Only nine new-build Brigands were delivered as T.4s (**WA561-WA569**), the rest of the fleet (33, to make a total of 42)

Brigand prototype MX988, the first of four prototypes ordered, made its maiden flight on 4 December 1944.

Above, Brigand prototype MX991 was used by the A&AEE for various trials between 1945 and 1947 as seen by the torpedo installed under the belly. Below, the third prototype (MX994). The man standing in front of the Brigand reveals the imposing size of the aircraft.

One of the few Brigand TF.1s built, RH748 is seen here with its full armament of a torpedo and four 60-lb rockets installed under each wing (not counting the four fixed 20mm cannon in the nose). The concept of carrying torpedoes for a strike was soon abandoned, eventually leading to the Brigand B.1. While the rockets were retained, the torpedo was replaced by a 2000-lb bomb, or two 1,000-lb, or 500-lb, bombs. The rockets could give way for one 500-lb bomb under each wing, but remained standard operational equipment.

was built up by converting B.1s. All T.4s were delivered by the end of 1951. They were equipped with the AI.10 radar, the same as installed on the Vampire NF.10, Venom NF.2 and Meteor NF.11. After three years the final variant, the Brigand T.5, appeared with a different AI installation in a slightly longer nose. This was necessary as new radars were introduced, like the AI.21 installed on the Venom NF.3 and Meteor NF.12 and NF.14. No new T.5s were built as all were converted B.1s supplemented by converted T.4s (23 in all).

THE MALAYAN EMERGENCY

The post-war years were plagued by various post-colonial wars and the British Empire had its share of trouble. The first skirmishes in Malaya arose in 1948 and only gained in intensity. In June 1948 the colonial government declared a state of emergency in British Malaya after the Malayan National Liberation Army, a communist guerrilla force, began murdering plantation workers. They wanted to free Malaya from British colonial rule. Many of the MNLA fighters were former members of the Malayan Peoples' Anti-Japanese Army who had been trained and funded by the British to fight the Imperial Japanese Army during the Second World War. Its political power was derived from landless, mostly communist, Malaysian Chinese 'squatters' who lived in poor dwellings between the commercial plantations and the jungle. After the MNLA had established a series of jungle bases, it began attacking British colonial government targets and Commonwealth military installations. It also sabotaged equipment as well as attacked workers and villages associated with the rubber plantation industry. Very quickly the guerrillas created large areas under communist control in the central areas of Malaya. In response to the MNLA the British colonial government launched a series of military counteroffensives. The operational tactics of the Commonwealth troops created the military term 'search and destroy', with the support of aircraft, the RAF providing the bulk of the squadrons based in the region. Rapid response units were established, that could react quickly to any guerrilla attacks, and volunteer forces were raised to guard towns and plantations. A programme of land reform, an attempt to placate the squatters, was also introduced to give entitlement to the land on which homes were built. Provincial governments built fortified villages to protect workers from raids. After more than twelve years the guerillas were living in such poor conditions they did not present a serious threat and the state of emergency was declared over in July 1960. In those twelve years many types served in support of the ground troops and that's where the Bristol Brigand saw its heaviest use.

Number of sorties: +18

First operational sortie:
08.08.52
Last operational sortie:
20.08.52

Number of claims: *nil*

Total aircraft written-off: 11

Aircraft lost on operations: 1
Aircraft lost in accidents: 10

Squadron code letters:

-

COMMANDING OFFICERS

S/L Alastair McK S. STEEDMAN	RAF No. 123469	RAF	...	09.10.50
S/L Christopher R.A. FORSYTH	RAF No. 42983	RAF	09.10.50	xx.02.52
S/L John W. STEPHENS (†)	RAF No. 40028	RAF	xx.02.52	21.04.52
S/L David B. BRETHERTON	RAF No. 115776	RAF	xx.05.52	...

SQUADRON USAGE

When WW2 ended, this unit was based in India and flying Liberators. The post-war re-organisation led to various changes before it was based at Khormaksar, Aden, in September 1946. Now flying Mosquitos, it soon switched to the Hawker Tempest, but changes came on 23 April 1949 when the first Brigand, RH814, arrived at the squadron. Some former Tempest pilots had been sent to the UK to undertake a Brigand conversion course. Flown by F/O F.A. Partridge, RH814 had entered the circuit when Partridge was asked over the R/T to fly round the area several times before landing. Misinterpreting the request, Partridge made a low run across the airfield from east to west, followed by another run from north to south. Unfortunately, on this second run, he struck a radio mast with the left wing tip, causing considerable damage to it and the aileron. He managed to keep control of the Brigand, but, per Murphy's Law – if it can go wrong, it will go wrong – the undercarriage refused to come down, even using the emergency system, so the Brigand made the landing on its belly, putting an end to its short flying career with 8 Squadron. The crew escaped without injuries. The squadron had to wait two more months, to July 1949, before other Brigands showed up (VS839 and VS856). At that time the squadron was commanded by Squadron Leader Alasdair McK. S. Steedman. The first Brigand flight took place on the 8th, with the CO at the controls, but an instrument failure forced an early return. The rest of the month was occupied with flight testing, with special focus on the cannons, but little flying was carried out in July, the total time barely exceeding twenty hours. This increased to 38 in August, but the month was plagued by technical issues with the engines and propellers. Otherwise, a third Brigand, VS819, was taken on charge and tested on the 30th. In September the squadron was engaged in operations against Yemeni who were building a post within the Western Protectorate territory border, but all actions carried out were flown by Tempests, the Brigand not yet being operational. However the type was ready enough to fly to Mogadiscio (Mogadishu) in Italian Somaliland for a three day stay from the 21st. Three Brigands contributed valuable air support by providing peaceful sweeps and recces over a wide area of unrest. It was the CO who commanded the detachment. The presence of the Brigands helped to restore order. This was done without any technical incidents and, on return to base, night flights began. A fourth Brigand, RH827, was air tested on the 8th and made serviceable.

The squadron returned to Mogadiscio on 7 October with two Brigands. This was in support of the civil power in Somalia during UN discussions on its future. The CO led the detachment again. The next day a third Brigand arrived, followed by two more on the 9th, to bring the detachment up to full strength (RH777, RH795, RH822, RH827 and VS839). Over the following days shows of force were carried out over almost all the towns of Somalia, ceasing on the 13th. The CO returned to Khormaksar on the 12th, relinquishing com-

A line up of 8 Sqn Brigands still painted in the colours they received in England. In the foreground is VS862/M, which would later make a belly-landing in April 1951 and be written off. *(A. Thomas)*

mand of the detachment to F/L Butt. The rest of the month was spent flying reconnaissance sorties and to wave the flag over potential hot spots. In all, the Brigands flew 65 hours on operations in October, 95 more being flown during training. Throughout November the squadron continued to maintain a force of three or four Brigands at Mogadiscio. The situation was, in general, more stable than in October and few sorties were flown, amounting to just thirty hours. Aside from the operational sorties, the detachment continued its training and, due to the presence of HMS *Birmingham*, a large number of naval co-operation exercises were carried out. The detachment was maintained until 12 December. However, the return was characterised by a lack of spare parts that limited air activity. Training continued, but 1949 ended in the worst manner when VS839 was posted missing from a night cross-country on the 30th. The navigation plan was to fly from Khormaksar to Perim Island, and then to an island near the port of Assab, Eritrea, before a return to base. The aircraft was lost without trace except for three dinghies found at various positions north of Perim Island. The search was finally abandoned on 6 January 1950. The cause of the death of the crew of four was never explained except it was clear the Brigand had hit the sea. In January 1950 the squadron remained at readiness for a possible move to Italian Somaliland. The Brigands were called once, with two aircraft, to show the flag in support of ground troops opposing tribesmen responsible for the looting of a yacht. The first fortnight of February was spent waiting on the call to go to Mogadiscio, therefore training was minimal to avoid using the few hours allotted each month. The order for the move eventually came on the 15th and four Brigands were sent on detachment on the 16th, later followed by two Dakotas carrying the groundcrew and equipment. The detachment ended on 27 March. During that time eighty hours were flown, but only eighteen of these were for 'waving the flag' or reconnaissance, the remainder being for training flights. The rest of the squadron saw its activity reduced and only 48 hours were flown. The detachment returned to base on 1 April after a short stay at Nairobi, Kenya. However, the squadron was already preparing to send another detachment of two Brigands to Asmara, Eritrea. These ultimately left on the 6th. Therefore, as efforts were made for this detachment, flying activity remained low at base. At Asmara, the detachment remained fully occupied flying daily reconnaissance and intimidation sorties over troubled areas of Eritrea. It was found the Brigand, owing to its weight and speed, was far from ideal for reconnaissance flights over terrain of this nature. However, the detachment flew nineteen sorties in April. Flying remained restricted at Khormaksar, but concentrated on continuing the conversion of newly arrived pilots. At Asmara, the mission remained the same and nineteen more sorties were completed, but the detachment returned at the end of May. At the beginning of June, five sorties were flown from Khormaksar to maintain communications with the Aden Protectorate, and also just to show the flag, but, generally speaking, training was limited by a lack of spares, four Brigands being grounded for the whole month for this reason. Routine was the key word for the following weeks, but the squadron continued to be hampered by the spares shortage, leading to a critical situation. In July, an average of six Brigands were continuously unserviceable during the month, and the Buckmaster was not available either. With the absorption of the Aden Protectorate Support Flight and its

Anson on 21 July, the Brigands and the Buckmaster were gathered in A Flight. In September A Flight spent part of the month at Nicosia for an Armament Practice Course, which was completed on 21 September. At Nicosia, Brigand RH795 was wrecked on the 8th when the pilot had to abandon the take off. The aircraft ran off the side of the runway and was badly damaged. After investigation it was struck off charge at the end of the month. A new CO, S/L C.R.A. Forsyth, took over in October. Flying at home in November was restricted once more to conserve hours for the detachment at Habbaniya. The move was initiated on the 28th for a two-week period. Its task would remain the same, 'air police' over the region and photography. It also served as fighter affiliation for No. 6 Squadron, flying Vampires, and No. 7 Squadron, of the RIraqAF, flying Hawker Furies. The detachment left Habbaniya on the 18th for Aden where the routine resumed until the end of the year.

This continued in 1951 with few events to mention other than some rare demonstration flights. The squadron flew its allotted number of hours monthly (about 160) during the first four months of the year. During this period Brigand RH818 suffered an undercarriage collapsed on landing on 20 February. The crew was safe, but the Brigand was written off one week later. The 160 hours was also reached in April, but another Brigand was written off that month after the undercarriage did not lower on return from dive bombing practice. Despite the best efforts of the pilot, a wheels-up landing became the only solution. Too damaged, VS862 was stricken at the end of the month after an investigation. At the end of May, A Flight was sent to RAF Shaibah initially for an armament practice camp, but the detachment ceased on 7 September after close to 500 hours flown. In this period of time two Brigands were written off, the first on 4 July when the undercarriage of VS814 did not lock down and another wheels-up landing was made. It was initially thought the aircraft could be repaired, but it was declared beyond economical repair on 12 October and struck off charge. This incident was followed soon after, on 16 July, by yet another undercarriage failure and yet another wheels-up landing. Brigand RH852 met the same fate as VS814 and was struck off charge on the same date. The rest of the year proved uneventful.

In February 1952, a detachment of six Brigands and one Buckmaster was sent to Nicosia for an armament practice camp, a long trip that saw each aircraft log ten hours. The returned journey was organised early in April, but was plagued by various technical issues during the trip, which began one aircraft short as it had become unserviceable just before departure. Two more could not take off from Khartoum during a stopover and completed the trip later on. A few days later, the squadron mourned the death of S/L Stephens DFC & Bar, the new CO, who was killed in a flying accident in a Buckmaster on 21 April. In May the decline of world petrol production caused a considerable impact on flying hours for the squadron, with just 100 hours allocated. Consequently, the ground training programme was accentuated. This limitation was, however, lifted in June. That month a detachment of three aircraft paid a visit to the Royal Ethiopian Air Force at Bishoftu and Jijiga between the 9th and 14th, but, outside that event, the routine remained the rule, as it did for

The black paint was found to be unsuitable for the climate at Aden and was altered to a gloss white on the upper surfaces. Here is another line-up of 8 Sqn Brigands, with white upper surfaces, but at the end of their career at Aden. In the foreground is RH812/D with RH827/F, VS816/A, and aircraft 'K' behind. *(Andrew Thomas)*

July, but, on the 23rd the Brigand fleet was suddenly grounded after a technical fault in the airframe on one of them was discovered. Air activity resumed on 7 August, but with restrictions imposed by the Air Ministry, with regard to aircraft handling, until the structural failures in the airframe had been rectified. In the meantime, however, a major incident had occurred on 24 July when a lorry was looted by members of a local tribe and, as it was the not the first time this kind of event had occurred in the area, involving the same people, a police action was decided. The situation degenerated on the ground and one Brigand was sent on a reconnaissance flight, flown by F/L Curd, on the 8th as soon as the grounding was lifted. The Brigand, flying low, was slightly damaged by ground fire. The sortie was repeated the following day, and leaflets were dropped, but this time the aircraft did not encounter any fire from the ground. As the situation remained unresolved, the British authorities decided to respond more firmly and air action was ordered against the village where the offenders had found shelter. On the 20th, S/L D.B. Bretherton DFC, the CO since May, took off at 06.00 and flew to the target to drop messages giving the offenders a final warning to be clear of their houses. Flight Lieutenant Curd, leading three rocket-armed Brigands, followed an hour later. Because the first assault didn't give the results expected, the target was attacked throughout the day until 17.00 when visibility and weather began to deteriorate rapidly. One Brigand, flown P/O C.P. Pratt (RH793), experienced difficulties with the undercarriage and the pilot carried out a range of measures to get the undercarriage to cycle properly. All attempts were unsuccessful, so Pratt fired his rockets and emptied his guns out at sea and landed the aircraft wheels up. It was struck off charge on 30 September after an investigation. In all, eighteen sorties were flown for this operation and 144 rockets fired, but only forty hit the targets. On 4 September another Brigand, RH777, sustained serious damage when it struck the ground heavily after the undercarriage collapsed. The aircraft was not repairable and the same misasdventure happened to RH792 on 13 October returning from a Navex. The rest of the year proved uneventful, except in December. Early that month it was announced the unit would re-equip with Vampires and preparations to receive the jets began. On 6 December, Sgt Dalton, captain of VS856, flew to Kamaran Island to uplift squadron personnel detached there to service the Vampires expected to stage through. After take off on the return flight, the right engine failed and Dalton returned to Kamaran Island, but he soon discovered only one wheel had lowered. A crash landing followed, but, fortunately, without consequences for the crew or passengers. For the Brigand, however, it was the end of its career and it was struck off charge the next month. Conversion training was initiated with a Gloster Meteor and the first hours on Vampires were soon logged. The bulk of the air activity remained with the Brigands, however, on which 132 hours were flown that month. Conversion training continued in January and the Brigands saw little flying that month. In February no hours was flown on the type, while, on the 21st, a signal was received ordering all Brigands to be scrapped on site.

Brigand VS816 was taken on 8 Sqn charge in January 1950. It served as aircraft 'A' until the squadron relinquished the type in February and it was struck off charge immediately after. Note the two spinners have been disposed of while the aircraft seems not to be under maintenance. It is not known why this was done.
(Andrew Thomas)

Date	Crew	S/N	Origin	Serial	Code	Fate
20.08.52	P/O Clifford P. **PRATT** *Rest of the crew unknown but safe.*	RAF No. 582797	RAF	**RH793**		-

Total: 1

Summary of the aircraft lost by accident - 8 Squadron

Date	Crew	S/N	Origin	Serial	Code	Fate
23.04.49	F/O Frederic A. **PARTRIDGE** *Rest of the crew unknown but safe.*	RAF No. 58989	RAF	**RH814**		-
30.12.49	F/O Desmond L. **SCOTT**	RAF No. 3036637	RAF	**VS839**	W	†
	N. III Peter W. **CROSS**	RAF No. 579191	RAF			†
	S. II Lionel V. **HAYES**	RAF No. 1894918	RAF			†
	One passenger, AC.2 D. Martin was also killed					
08.09.50	P/O John C. **ATKINSON** *Rest of the crew unknown but safe.*	RAF No. 607004	RAF	**RH795**		-
20.02.51	F/L Ernest J.R. **DOWNS** *Rest of the crew unknown but safe.*	RAF No. 58691	RAF	**RH818**		-
10.04.51	F/Sgt William T. **McLARTY** *Rest of the crew unknown but safe.*	RAF No. 656069	RAF	**VS862**	M	-
04.07.51	Sgt Frank G. **ALLEN** *Rest of the crew unknown but safe.*	RAF No. 3046099	RAF	**VS814**		-
16.07.51	F/O Edward N. **BARRINGTON-R.** *Rest of the crew unknown but safe.*	RAF No. 607040	RAF	**RH852**		-
16.07.51	P/O John R. **CHATHAM** *Rest of the crew unknown but safe.*	RAF No. 4040470	RAF	**RH777**		-
13.10.52	Sgt **GILES** *Rest of the crew unknown but safe.*	RAF No. ?	RAF	**RH792**		-
06.12.52	F/Sgt Raymond J.R. **DALTON** *Rest of the crew unknown but safe.*	RAF No. 1328186	RAF	**VS856**		-

Total: 10

8 Squadron's Brigands flying in formation. Below, a close up of VS835/M from the same formation.
(Andrew Thomas)

Number of sorties: *ca.* 1,600

First operational sortie:
19.12.49
Last operational sortie:
07.02.52

Number of claims: *nil*

Total aircraft written-off: 4

Aircraft lost on operations: 3
Aircraft lost in accidents: 1

Squadron code letters:
OB

COMMANDING OFFICERS

S/L Edward D. CREW	RAF No. 74700	RAF	...	13.02.50
S/L Alexander C. BLYTHE	RAF No. 66567	RAF	13.02.50	27.08.51
S/L Ian S. STOCKWELL	RAF No. 132080	RAF	27.08.51	...

SQUADRON USAGE

Based in the Far East from early 1942 onwards, 45 squadron had been sent to reinforce the RAF in the region after the Japanese invasion. At the end of war it was equipped with Bristol Beaufighters and was involved in the early stages of the communist insurrection in Malaya in August 1948. For this purpose the squadron had moved to Kuala Lumpur, via Butterworth, in May 1949 and was commanded by S/L E.D. Crew who had commanded a Mosquito unit during the war (No. 96 Squadron). The Beaufighter was, however, an obsolete aircraft at the end of the forties and, after seven months of operations, the squadron began to convert to the Brigand B.1 and Met.3, even though the latter would soon form a separate unit (see later Met.3 text).

The first Brigand, VS857, landed at Kuala Lumpur on 6 September. It soon went off to Singapore for a more suitably sized airfield and would be officially taken on charge at Tengah by a detachment of the squadron which had been set up to support the introduction of the new type. Two more Brigands (VS813 and VS832) were received at Tengah in November with their posted crews while orders were received to move to that base from 12 December to complete conversion. The squadron continued its operations on Beaufighters from Tengah while conversion was underway on the Brigand and the Buckmaster. On 16 December the first incident was reported when, during a training flight, F/O Neil's aircraft experienced a propeller overspeed, but managed to land safely on one engine. Three more Brigands (RH829, VS855 and VS864) arrived in December, bringing 45's strength up to six examples. The baptism of fire for the Brigand with 45 occurred on the 19th when one accompanied four Beaufighters on a strike to the north east of Kallang. Strikes continued in January 1950 with eight sorties flown of the 51 recorded by the squadron. Most efforts were still devoted, however, to the completion of the conversion programme. While some incidents were recorded, none were very serious. The squadron flew its last Beaufighter sortie on 7 February 1950, leaving the Brigand to do the job. Ten days later a change of command took place, S/L A.C. Byrthe (DFC) assuming command from the 13th. February was quiet with only nine sorties flown on the type. Practice flights continued at the same time and, in all, 185 hours on Brigands, and twenty more Buckmaster hours, were flown in February. Two raids were flown in March on the 19th, with six Brigands and on the 27th with five aircraft. A third raid was aborted on the 31st due to low cloud over the target and the bombs were jettisoned in to the sea. With the various practice flights carried out during the month, the six Brigands logged about 210 hours, but 45 came close to a major setback when, on the 19th, during the attack, one of the delayed-action 500-lb bombs the CO was carrying detonated shortly after it had been released, fortunately causing only superficial damage. In April eighteen strikes and one convoy escort were flown for a total of 75 sorties. On the 4th the squadron carried the Brigand's full bomb load for the first time with two 1000 pounders, two 500-lb bombs and rockets and cannons deployed. A few days later, on the 15th Pilot II M. Clarke lost pressure in the left engine. He feathered the prop, jettisoned his bombs and made a successful landing on one engine. A similar experien-

Squadron Leader A.C. Blythe in Brigand RH829/OB-M leading a formation over typical Malayan jungle. Finding and attacking targets was most difficult, otherwise there was no opposition of any kind. *(Andrew Thomas)*

ce occurred a few days later to F/L A.P. Norman who had his right engine start to overspeed. He was obliged to jettison his bombs out to sea and experienced trouble feathering the prop. Height was difficult to maintain and he landed short without flaps to avoid losing more height. May was also intense with 53 sorties, which saw the delivery of 84 1000-lb bombs, 82 500-lb bombs, 243 60-lb rockets and 23,000 rounds of 20mm. This achievement was repeated in June over 64 sorties. The squadron was facing technical issues with the 20mm cannons, because of their poor state, and the armourers had a hard time trying to keep them operational. Therefore, in order to alleviate the workload, only two cannons per aircraft were used during each sortie that month. The number of sorties increased to 81 in July, but that month also saw the loss of a Brigand (RH850) on the 6th when it crashed during a strike. The aircraft was seen to hit the top of a hill while launching its rockets. It disintegrated and burst into flames. Considering the nature of the spot, thick jungle, it was considered impractical to send a search party. In August, the cannon issue was solved by replacing barrels after they had fired 500 rounds. This limited the number of stoppages and permitted an additional 10,000 rounds to be loosed off compared to July. That issue was solved, but another appeared when it was found that carrying two 1000-lb bombs was cracking the skins of the aircraft behind the nose. That led to a change of the load, initially replacing one of the two 1000-lb bombs with one 500 pounder and, at the end of the year, by the use of 500-lb bombs only. Until the end of the year, more than 230 hours were flown with no major events to report.

January 1951 started badly when a second Brigand, VS838, crashed during a strike on the 11th. Of the crew, only the pilot, Sgt Hayler, managed to bale out. The cause of this loss was an explosion in the cannon bay as the aircraft was leveling out. The Brigand caught fire and became uncontrollable. Sadly, while the location of Hayler was precisely known, it took five days for the rescue team to reach him. By that time he had died. The same cause led to the same results one month later when VS859 crashed at Pilah, killing the two men on board. Fortunately, the crew consisted of two, not the usual three, but that loss led to an immediate embargo on the further use of guns pending investigation. The two-man crew had become necessary at the beginning of 1951 due to the shortage of navigators within the squadron. Since most ops were flown in formation, only a navigator in the lead aircraft was needed to conduct the aircraft to the target. As for the gun issue, after an investigation and various trials, the ban was lifted in April, but with firing restricted to short bursts and only ball ammunition to be employed (high explosive ammunition was prohibited). March, April and May were free of any major events despite more than 220 sorties carried out, including close to 100 in May. The squadron could have been excused for thinking its run of bad luck was behind it, but that was soon proved wrong. On 15 June the right engine of VS857 fell off during an air test, causing the aircraft to crash among the mangroves just to the north of Tengah. The signaler, Sgt P. Weston, initially attempted to bale out, but realised the aircraft was too low. Sergeant Martin, hoping that he might reach the runway, had lowered the undercarriage legs and these, still partially extended, caused the Brigand to somersault onto its back and slide along Kranji Creek upside down. The nose cone broke off and the pilot emerged through the hole. Weston escaped through the lower hatch, which was now the upper hatch. Having first helped the injured Martin to dry land, the signaler realised their navigator was missing. Sergeant P. Weston went back to look for him, but by this time the aircraft had filled up with muddy water and he could not get back into the crew compartment to attempt a rescue and, sadly, Sgt V. Bowen was lost. Since No. 84 Squadron had previously lost a Brigand in similar circumstances (on 1 June) and would lose another one on the 19th, the whole Brigand fleet was grounded. The cause of these accidents was eventually traced to the fracturing of the Rotol propellers around the blade roots after about 400 hours of running time. The prop would throw a blade and the subsequent vibration would tear the engine off its bearers. Consequently, new engine bearers and new propellers were fitted and the aircraft were restored to service. The squadron resumed operations on 12 July when the CO participated in a sortie in conjunction with 84 Squadron. Therefore, the number of sorties in July was limited to 25. That month most of the raids were flown in conjunction with 84. Again, they were few, but, in the same period, hydraulic serviceability caused headaches for the mechanics and it was not until the end of the month that 45 could count on five Brigands. In August the number of sorties was doubled across 22 raids despite the recurrent issues with the undercarriage and its hydraulics (although there were some improvements in availability). During August a change of command took place, with the arrival of S/L I.S. Stockwell from the UK, to replace S/L A.C Blythe from the 27th. That month also saw the first use of the two-tier rocket mounting, permitting the Brigand to carry and launch up to sixteen 60-lb rockets. This somewhat compensated for the lack of firepower since the guns had been inhibited again due to an incident in 84 Squadron early in the month. This latest ban on the guns remained until February 1952. In September operational tasking declined and no operations was carried out between the 17th and 30th. In October operational activity, as well as training, was increased, the only concern being the only Buckmaster on hand flying less than ten hours and suffering three emergency landings! During the month 45 maintained a detachment at Butterworth, under the command of F/L Muth, for the first fourteen days and flew nineteen sorties. In November 144 sorties were achieved. This was a record for 45, but also for any Brigand unit in the region. That followed the assassination of Sir Henry Gurney, the British High Commissioner in Malaya. The record was achieved because 45's strength had risen to ten Brigands and allowed the deployment of 4-5 aircraft at Kuala Lumpur. In December 84 Squadron relieved 45 at Kuala Lumpur, where the latter was present between the 13th and 18th only, and the number of sorties dropped to 37.

Brigand Is VS864/OB-N and VS865/OB-R flying over Johore Strait in the early 1950s. While VS864 was struck off charge in October 1952, VS865 survived to become a Brigand T.4, then a T.5, and would serve with 238 OCU as a trainer. It was eventually struck off charge in March 1958.

In January and February 1952 the squadron sent a detachment to Kuala Lumpur and stayed there for a month between 11 January and 11 February. During those two months about 125 sorties were carried out with the following armament expenditure: 26 1000-lb bombs, 284 500-lb bombs, 1319 60-lb rockets and 4185 20mm shells. In the beginning of the year, personnel were notified the unit would convert to the DH Hornet. The first machines arrived at the end of January with some Mosquitos for training purposes. The final strike by Brigands was carried out on 7 February and the very last sortie was flown the following day. This last sortie was in support of the employment of paratroopers for the first time in Malaya since the 'emergency' began. The record for the Brigand era with 45 was not too bad with close to 1600 sorties carried out against the insurgents representing 3500 hours of flight. More than 10,000 rockets were launched with 1400 tons of bombs dropped and 285,600 rounds of ammunition fired.

Summary of the aircraft lost on Operations - 45 Squadron

Date	Crew	S/N	Origin	Serial	Code	Fate
06.07.50	F/O Norman B. **Harben**	RAF No. 2238185	RAF	**RH850**	OM-U	†
	N. II Tom W. **Smith**	RAF No. 578704	RAF			†
	S. III Clifford **Lloyd**	RAF No. 578681	RAF			†
11.01.51	Sgt Sydney V. **Hayler**	RAF No.579267	RAF	**VS838**	OM-A	†
	Sgt George A. **Robinson**	RAF No. 3032204	RAF			†
	Sgt Kenneth **Hall**	RAF No. 579330	RAF			†
15.02.51	Sgt William **Kent**	RAF No. 1852236	RAF	**VS859**	OM-G	†
	Sgt Bruce A. **Ellis**	RAF No. 3045992	RAF			†

Total: 3

Summary of the aircraft lost by accident - 45 Squadron

Date	Crew	S/N	Origin	Serial	Code	Fate
15.06.51	Sgt Alan J. **Martin**	RAF No. 1862795	RAF	**VS857**	OM-K	-
	Sgt Peter A. **Watson**	RAF No. 2209329	RAF			-
	Sgt Vernon **Bowden**	RAF No. 1654380	RAF			†

Total: 1

Number of sorties: *ca.* 1,650

First operational sortie:
14.04.50
Last operational sortie:
04.12.52

Number of claims: *nil*

Total aircraft written-off: 10

Aircraft lost on operations: 5
Aircraft lost in accidents: 5

Squadron code letters:

-

COMMANDING OFFICERS				
S/L Stanley G. NUNN	RAF No. 81935	RAF	...	16.09.49
S/L George C. UNWIN	RAF No. 46298	RAF	16.09.49	04.08.51
S/L Ayshford P. NORMAN	RAF No. 154774	RAF	04.08.51	15.07.52
S/L Lewis L. JOHNSTON	RAF No. 39463	(AUS)/RAF	15.07.52	23.01.53
F/L William MACLEOD (Temp.)	RAF No. 169010	RAF	23.01.53	20.02.53

SQUADRON USAGE

A long-term overseas RAF unit, 84 Squadron was among the few to be still involved in operational sorties when WW2 ceased in September 1945. It provided support to the Allied forces in Java in the autumn of 1945, flying Mosquitos at that time. The squadron returned to Singapore in May 1946 and converted to Bristol Beaufighters. In November 1948 it was sent to Habbaniya in Iraq where it was to be converted to Brigands. However, that phase was delayed and the first Brigands were only received in February 1949. The first pair (RH817 and RH818) was ferried direct from the UK, arriving from the 9th onwards, followed by RH810 and RH812. The last of the initial five, RH815, arrived on the 20th. The first flights were soon underway, the privilege of being first for 84 went to the CO, S/L S.G. Nunn, a former Beaufighter pilot during WW2. In March three more Brigands were added to the inventory (RH809, RH811 and RH813) and, in all, 84 flew 87.50 hours on Brigands, but no armament training flights could be performed due to a lack of rocket rails, RPs and practice bombs. At the same time more aircrew began to arrive to complete the crews as the Brigand had a crew of three, not two like the Beaufighter. In April the situation was about the same with another ninety hours flown, but the lack of spare parts began to impact on aircraft serviceability especially once inspections revealed problems with the hydraulics. One aircraft due for inspection was, therefore, temporarily used to provide parts for the others. At last, in May, some armament practice could be done, and a good 114 hours were flown, while, in June, hydraulics caused much trouble. In the middle of the month, the squadron was requested to show the flag over towns and villages in Trucial Oman (a group of tribal confederations in the south-eastern corner of the Arabian peninsula), where some slave trading had been noticed, to oblige locals to respect the treaties signed previously. If we ignore that, training continued as usual. Serviceability in July and August was bad and, altogether, just 130 hours were flown during those two months. In September a change of command took place when S/L G.C. Unwin, a veteran of the Battle of Britain, arrived on the 6th. Serviceability improved that month and also saw the arrival of RH826/J and RH828/K fitted with metal-bladed propellers. The latter aircraft fell victim to a training accident a few days later when it hit the water during a low-level flight, damaging the propellers. Fortunately the pilot, F/O Bakker, managed to return base. This was the first incident, involving a Brigand, for 84. In October, however, more problems arose. Cracks in the skin on the undersurfaces of the mainplane, and wrinkles on the upper surfaces, were found on two aircraft. They were grounded and the damage found to be caused by excessive g-forces during armament exercises. However, the pilots had flown their aircraft well under their limits and never exceeded 3.5 g on any occasion. Consequently, restrictions were imposed on all aircraft

Photo of poor quality but interesting showing some of the first Brigands issued to 84 Sqn flying some training sorties over the desert landscape of Somaliland. In the foreground is RH818/B, which would leave the squadron after an accident sustained on 19 November 1949. Repaired, it was allocated to 8 Sqn with which it was lost on 20 February 1950. The other two aircraft are RH817/A, wrecked on 9 March 1950, and RH815/E, destroyed during a practice flight in Malaya on 31 July 1950. *(A.Thomas)*

and no dive bombing could be performed. In November Brigands RH818 and RH826, the two which had cracks, were flown back to the UK to be investigated by engineers of Bristol, but cracks were soon found on RH817. Despite this, the number of hours flown by Brigands was satisfactory in November and December with over 130 hours flown each month. On 28 December the restrictions were partially lifted, allowing 300 kts and 2 g. In January 1950 the cracking issues were solved and modifications undertaken. This was accompanied by new flying techniques to be used when carrying armament. Now, being at full operational status, the squadron was put on stand-by for moving four Brigands to Mogadiscio in Italian Somaliland to provide air support. The move eventually took place on 26 February. The aircraft were RH809/F, RH810/C, RH813/H and RH815/E under the command of F/L D.W. Smith. In March the Brigands faced another restriction to flying, imposed from the 8th, to conserve hours in preparation for the detachment of the squadron to Tengah in Malaya but on 9th March 1950, Brigand RH817 flown by F/L D.W. Smith had hydraulic pump failure and could not get the undercarriage to lock down even by using the hand-pump and after cutting a hole in the hydraulic tank using the escape axe and pouring in water, having no more alternative but to belly-land. On the 25th the four Brigands, which were temporarily based at Mogadiscio, returned to Habbaniya having flown 136 hours (including the ferry time), but no operations. The few flights consisted of photography of strategic points, message dropping, testing of wireless communications with Army units, and reporting on the state of the weather and roads. On 22 March RH816 and RH823 were allotted to the squadron and collected.

The move to the South East Asia began on 4 April with four Brigands – RH828/K, RH823/A, RH811/H and RH813/H – followed by four more the next day (RH816/B, RH809/F, RH815/E and RH810/C). They arrived at Singapore on the 8th. Six days after their arrival the first strike against the insurgents was carried out with six aircraft each carrying four 500-lb bombs, six 60-lb RPs and 800 rounds of ammunition. On the 15th and 16th targets in the same area were attacked, six and five aircraft being employed respectively. Strikes would become the routine from now on. On the 21st RH816 was specially modified for a PR mission on request of Operations Kuala Lumpur and, during the last eight days of the month, strikes were intensified. On the 24th the squadron dropped 1000-lb bombs in the Kuantan area, the first time such bombs were dropped from a Brigand. At the end of the month 84 could attest to having dropped 151,000 pounds of bombs, fired 390 RPs and expended 45,375 rounds of 20mm in 68 sorties. In May 65 sorties were flown during which 141,000 pounds of bombs were dropped, 287 RPs launched and 25,292 rounds fired. From now the squadron entered a new routine, achieving around 60-75 sorties per month, all but a few being strikes against ground targets (the rest being escorts of some kind). On 31 July, while escorting a convoy of schoolchildren from their school in the Cameron Highlands to Tapah, RH815, flown by F/L D.C. Marshall, flight CO, and his crew, was seen to crash into hilly jungle at the side of the road. All three on board were killed. The

Mission accomplished! Four Brigands returning quietly from a strike sortie over Malaya, having fired their rockets at a target. Visible in the photo are RH811/G, lost on 19 June 1951 returning from a strike, VS861/B and RH831/E. The latter was sent back to the UK, following an overhaul, where it was converted to a T.5. It was eventually lost in an accident on 8 March 1956. Its aircraft letter 'E' was taken over by RH755.

reasons for the accident remained obscure, but the weather, which was very poor at that time, could be the main reason. Misfortune continued in August when two accidents were recorded – RH823 on the 9th and RH816 on the 12th. While for RH823 there were no serious implications and the aircraft was repaired, this was not the case for RH816. Pilot II Hickson, returning from a strike in the Setul area, attempted to overshoot, but pulled the flaps and undercarriage too soon and the Brigand sank into the ground and crashed. No one on board was hurt, but the aircraft was a write-off. During the next few weeks, serviceability decreased mainly due to the recurrent hydraulic problem, which grounded many Brigands. In November two more Brigands were written-off. On the 9th RH828, the CO's 'Queen of Shaibah', was on a non-operational flight being collected back from Butterworth by Sgt Limbert and made a flapless landing at Seletar, but experienced brake failure once on the runway. Trying to avoid running off the end of the runway, he swung the aircraft on to the grass, hoping this would act as a brake. Unfortunately the Brigand went in to a ditch hidden in the grass. The aircraft folded up and one of the oleo legs came up though the wing. Nobody was hurt. The second accident occurred on the 20th when a bomb fell off its rack during take off for a strike. The bomb bounced off the runway and hit the underside of the fuselage forward of the tail unit of RH809. Fortunately, it did not explode. The Brigand was sent to the MU where it was eventually struck off charge. December saw a reduction of activity owing to a lack of strikes during the first nine days, a practice flypast for the Singapore Air Display and the onset of the festive season. Less than fifty sorties were flown, making a total of more than 600 sorties, since the arrival of the squadron in Malaya, during which 1360 500-lb bombs were dropped, 3167 RPs launched and 219,146 rounds of 20mm expended. A little less than 2000 hours were also In January 1951 heavy rainfall prevented much flying and, in all, 75 sorties were carried out during which 140,000 pounds of bombs were dropped, 42 RPs and 20,727 rounds of 20mm fired. In February seventy more sorties were performed. When the squadron celebrated the first anniversary of its presence in South East Asia, more than 3000 hours of flight had been logged. April '51 was quiet, but, with two new aircraft arriving that month, RH796 and VS869, 84 now had ten Brigands on May saw the unit's peak of activity with more than 400 hours flown. The squadron dropped its 200,000th pound of bombs since arrival. May also saw the first time the squadron put eight Brigands over one target at the same time, this 'first' occurring on the 28th. Others would soon follow. June saw two dramatic events occur. On the 1st Brigand VS869 crashed during a training flight, killing the three crew. Later, on the 19th, RH811 was lost after an engine failure returning from a strike. The pilot escaped by parachute, but, unfortunately the navigator did not leave the aircraft. As 45 Squadron had encountered a similar accident with one of its Brigands, the decision was taken to ground all examples pending a full investigation. The ban was lifted on 7 July, the date the first aircraft returning from the modification centre became available. The next operational sortie took place on the 12th. During the month, the squadron received new propellers and engine bearers and six aircraft received mods to their hydraulics. Having been cut almost in half, only 41 sorties were carried out in July. In August other problems arose when cannon usage was halted. That occurred on the 5th after a violent explosion, following a strafing

A crewmember inspecting the rockets just loaded on to RH823/P by the mechanics ahead of another sortie over the jungle. The Brigand is also armed with a single 500-lb bomb under the belly.

Brigand RH776/K, leading, with RH755/E on its right, is preparing to conduct a RP attack on a target located in the middle of jungle.

attack, was felt by one of the pilots. At base it was found the blast tube of the port outer gun had burst as the gun was fired. At the end of the month, the squadron lost its CO, when he was sent to the UK for medical repatriation after breaking his leg, who was replaced by F/L A.P. Norman. Activity was low in September, the lowest since the unit's arrival in Malaya, not one operation was even carried out during the ten days between the 14th and the 23rd. The squadron also sent a detachment to Butterworth for two weeks until 5 October, a month that saw operational activity increase. There was nothing to report until the end of the year when Brigands were sent at Kuala Lumpur to respond with immediate strikes, but few calls were made. In January 1952 operations were limited by two factors, the aftermath of the festive season and extensive flooding over most of the highlands in the Federation. Actually, most of the 53 sorties that month were flown by the Kuala Lumpur detachment, which was back at base on the 11th. The number of sorties increased in February, 84 participating in three large operations, which included an airborne landing on the border of Siam (Thailand) while another detachment was sent to Kuala Lumpur. March was also seen as a good month with 86 sorties carried out during which 779 60-lb rockets were fired, 78,500 pounds of bombs dropped, and 16,752 cannon rounds expended. In March good news came when it was made known the previous OC, S/L Unwin, had been awarded the DSO for his service with the squadron in Malaya. A reorganisation also took place, the squadron now being made up of two flights, even though the establishment didn't change with ten Brigands and one Buckmaster on hand. Then came the idea to ease administrative duties with an almost permanent detachment at Kuala Lumpur. During April 78 sorties were flown by the squadron. The weight of bombs dropped reached 47,000 lbs, the number of rockets fired was 1202 and 20mm ammunition expended came to 24,587 rounds. For the first time during the squadron's presence in Malaya, it was used operationally at night. On the first day of May all of 84's aircraft and crews were dispatched at Kuala Lumpur for Operation Biterbit. This required two Brigands to maintain a patrol in the vicinity of Kuala Lumpur airfield, within R/T range, from dawn till dusk. A further two Brigands were placed on immediate readiness on the ground and the remainder were on standby. The idea was to give the usual pre-strike briefing by R/T to the crews on the 'Air Alert Mission' and so cut down the time interval between the demand for the strike and the aircraft arriving on target. Each crew was equipped with a complete set of target maps for Malaya and it was a simple matter for them to find the correct area and plot the target in the air.

It was anticipated the system would be justified by an increase in strikes due to the terrorists recently increasing their activity. However, this was not the case and, although the squadron did carry out a few strikes in record time, it was considered the operation was not a success as no enemy was reported killed. On 3 May the squadron suffered the loss of a crew on a strike near Chenderoh Lake in Perak. Eyewitnesses reported seeing the Brigand, RH755, commence a normal rocket attack. As the pilot was releasing his rockets, a flash was seen under the starboard wing of the aircraft and all, or part, of that wing fell away. The aircraft rolled over and crashed into the target, catching fire on impact. Later, on the 25th, the pilot of RH796 experienced severe vibration from the right engine so feathered the propeller immediately. A normal single engine landing was carried out at Kuala Lumpur, but, after touching down, the Brigand swung to the right towards a line of aircraft. In an endeavour to avoid these aircraft the undercarriage was overstressed, causing it to collapse. The Brigand was too damaged to consider any repair. June and July saw operational activity decreasing with sixteen sorties in July, the lowest so far. On 12 July there was a change of command, S/L L.L. Johnston, an Australian serving in the RAF and who had been awarded the DSO during the war while leading 458 Squadron, taking over the squadron from a tour-expired S/L Norman. August was also quiet with strikes taking place on the 7th, 8th, 13th, 26th, 28th and 30th for a total of 23 sorties. The first five days could not be flown as the Brigands were grounded during that time for examinations of their No. 1 fuel tank bays.

As far as operational flying was concerned, September was considered a good month with close to 100 sorties carried out. All but two were flown by the detachment of four Brigands at Kuala Lumpur. The bulk of those sorties took place after the 12th when a considerable number of requests for offensive support were made to cover Operation Peter, the neutralisation of various camps in the east part of the Tanjong Malim. It was reported eleven camps, two food dumps and other minor targets were eliminated. Early in October the Kuala Lumpur detachment returned to Tengah so, logically, the number of sorties decreased, in fact halved. With another detachment sent to Kuala Lumpur in November, 84 dropped 87,000 pounds of bombs, launched 566 RPs and fired 20,616 rounds of ammunition. Almost no operations were flown in December, only seventeen sorties, and the Kuala Lumpur detachment was assumed by 45 Squadron. The last two strike sorties were flown on the 4th. While only a few operations were flown, training continued. On the 20th, RH823 was lost with its crew. The crash occurred during a demonstration strike laid on for the *Somerset Light Infantry* who had recently arrived in Malaya. Two aircraft were detailed to carry out dive bombing and cannon attacks on selected targets in Jahore State near Kota Diggi. The first Brigand, VS861, carried out a normal dive bombing attack and was followed by RH823 in a similar attack. As RH823 commenced its recovery, the right wing was seen to break away. The aircraft continued in its dive and burst into flames on impact with the ground. It was later found that a structural failure was the cause of the crash. That came at the same time as rumours suggesting the end of the squadron's activities in Malaya, reduction to a cadre basis and a return to the UK. The squadron was stood down and only flights on Harvards were carried out. On 31 January 1953 the squadron was officially disbanded in Malaya with effect reported on 20 February. In all, 84 Squadron had carried out more than 1650 sorties in support of Commonwealth troops during its time in Malaya.

RH776/K in action with the rockets having just been launched, leaving a trail of smoke behind them. Rockets were the main weapon used by the Brigand in Malaya.

Summary of the aircraft lost on Operations - 84 Squadron

Date	Crew	S/N	Origin	Serial	Code	Fate
31.07.50	F/L Desmond C. **Marshall**	RAF No. 55252	RAF	**RH815**	E	†
	F/L Richard S. **Wrigglesworth**	RAF No. 167386	RAF			†
	S. III Paul **Blakey**	RAF No. 3039885	RAF			†
12.08.50	P. II George E. **Hickson**	RAF No. 3042144	RAF	**RH816**	B	-
	N. IV Terence **Stringer**	RAF No. 3504506	RAF			-
	P. III Michael R.H. **Alden**	RAF No. 3112987	RAF			-
	S. II Frederic W. **Bunning**	RAF No. 579006	RAF			-
20.11.50	S/L George C. **Unwin**	RAF No. 46298	RAF	**RH809**	F	-
	Rest of the crew not reported but safe					
19.06.51	F/O Ian S. **Macpherson**	RAF No. 607023	RAF	**RH811**	G	-
	F/O Ronald E. **Matthews**	RAF No. 133231	RAF			†
03.05.52	F/O Basil A.D. **Cochrane**	RAF No. 607110	RAF	**RH755**	E	†
	Sgt James B. **Armstrong**	RAF No. 4038565	RAF			†
	And one passenger, C.J.A. Cox was killed					

Total: 5

Summary of the aircraft lost by accident - 84 Sqn

Date	Crew	S/N	Origin	Serial	Code	Fate
09.03.50	F/L Derek W. **Smith**	RAF No. 193425	RAF	**RH817**	A	-
	Rest of the crew not reported but safe					
09.11.50	P.II Alan **Limbert**	RAF No. 3044684	RAF	**RH828**	K	-
01.06.51	F/O Keith J. **Fullagar**	RAF No. 2360054	RAF	**VS869**		†
	F/Sgt Harry L.P. **Gregory**	RAF No. 583395	RAF			†
	F/Sgt Charles **Sharkey**	RAF No. 550949	RAF			†
25.05.52	F/L Richard **Tuffin**	RAF No. 3062577	RAF	**RH796**		-
20.12.52	F/L Bredan **Massey**	RAF No. 146871	RAF	**RH823**	P	†
	Sgt Edward C. **Powell**	RAF No. 1580783	RCAF			†
	One passenger, an air mechanic, LAC D. Kay was also killed					

Total: 5

<u>No. 1301 Flight</u>

The Met.3 was an unarmed variant of the Brigand dedicated to meteorological flights at high altitude. These were fitted with special weather-recording equipment to allow them to monitor conditions in the upper atmosphere and supply data for the preparation of weather forecasts. The aircraft's structure was unchanged, but all of the weaponry and fittings were taken out including the gun channels. Long-range tanks, an oxygen system to allow the crew to fly at high altitudes, a sensitive high altitude altimeter, and extra radio equipment, as well, of course, as meteorological equipment and a psychrometer (a kind of thermometer), were installed. The de-icing system was also improved. The prototype of this version, RH763, was sent for conversion from its B.1 configuration a few days after its delivery to the RAF. It was tested at the A&AEE from February 1948 onwards and led to the delivery of the sixteen Brigand Met.3s between November 1948 and February 1949. The Met.3s were sent to Ceylon and incorporated initially, in May 1949, in to No. 45 Squadron. In that time a new unit, the recently reformed No. 1301 Flight, was established. Within a month the first three Met.3s (VS821, VS822 and VS824) were officially transferred to the new Flight at the time both Flights and 45 Squadron moved to Kuala Lumpur in Malaya. There it was joined by VS817 to bring its initial full complement to four Brigands. The Met.3s undertook daily sorties over the Indian Ocean, flown in a triangle in the direction of the prevailing monsoon. These began with a climb to about 1700 feet followed by a spiral climb to 25,000 feet in readiness for a 200-mile cruise at that altitude. Weather readings were taken every 50 miles (80 km) and then the Brigand would drop to sea level for its return home. No aircraft was ever lost during these sorties even though the Brigands were sometimes damaged in the severe weather conditions and turbulence. The Flight eventually ceased its activity in November 1951 when it was disbanded on the 30th after having recorded about 600 weather sorties. Of the sixteen production aircraft delivered, only six were actually issued to the Flight, the remaining aircraft being kept in reserve and never used.

A side view of VS820, one of the few Brigand Met.3s delivered to the RAF. This mark had a short career with the RAF.

<u>**Nos. 228 & 238 OCU**</u>

In the UK only the T.4/T.5s were used. The first unit to convert was No. 228 OCU, based at Leeming, replacing its obsolete Wellington T.18s from July 1951 onwards. In July 1952, as training requirements increased, the Brigands moved to Colerne to form part of No. 238 OCU, their section becoming the Airborne Interception School. The target aircraft used during the training sorties were Boulton Paul Balliol T.2s and a few Spitfire LF.16s. The first Brigand T.5s arrived in July 1954 and, in January 1957, 238 OCU moved to North Luffenham in Rutland while the surviving T.4s went back to 228 OCU at Leeming. Advances in technology were rapid and, by 1957, AI.10 operators were no longer needed for the new generation of fighters being introduced into service. Therefore, the need for Brigand T.5s diminished rapidly to the point that 238 OCU was disbanded on 17 March 1958. In all, about six hundred navigators received their training on the Brigand, which normally consisted of 45 hours on the type. A handful of Brigands also served with 236 OCU, a maritime training unit. Some accidents involving Brigand T.4/T.5s were recorded during that period as follows :

Date	Crew	S/N	Origin	Serial	Unit	fate
14.10.48	F/L Desmond C. **Marshall**	RAF No. 55252	RAF	**RH803**	228 OCU	-
16.01.51	P/O Peter F. **Keeling**	RAF No. 582152	RAF	**RH770**	228 OCU	-
	rest of the crew or passengers not reported but safe.					
23.02.53	F/L Alan A.J. **Symington**	RAF No. 180387	RAF	**RH760**	238 OCU	†
	F/Sgt Walter E. **Cox**	RAF No. 4117783	RAF			†
	P/O David **Wilmot**	RAF No. 2479597	RAF			†
	P/O William B. **Parker**	RAF No. 2523032	RAF			†
17.09.54	F/Sgt Raymond J.R. **Dalton**	RAF No. 1328186	RAF	**RH807**	238 OCU	-
	rest of the crew or passengers not reported but safe.					
02.09.55	F/Sgt G.F. **Lamb**	RAF No. 1113352	RAF	**RH768**	238 OCU	-
	rest of the crew or passengers not reported but safe.					
08.03.56	F/Sgt David W.H. **Hanson**	RAF No. 1545694	RAF	**RH831**	238 OCU	†
	F/O Ronald J. **Crocker**	RAF No. 3509882	RAF			†
	Lt K.E. **Varney**		RN			**Inj.**
	Lt N.R. **Auld**		RN			**Inj.**

Other Brigands were also victim of accident while serving with various non-operational units, mainly as test aircraft:

Date	Crew	S/N	Origin	Serial	Unit	fate
01.10.46	F/L Denis G.W. **Tayler**	RAF No. 141476	RAF	**RH744**	RAE	-
19.07.47	F/L Thomas W.G. **Morren**	RAF No. 48008	RAF	**RH752**	A&AEE	†
	F/L Ian J. **Hartley**	RAF No. 111978	RAF			†
12.10.51	F/L Stanley G. **Hewitt**	RAF No. 152251	RAF	**RH759**	19 MU	-
08.05.52	Lt D.P. **Norman**		RN	**RH773**	ATDU	-
02.07.52	F/L Gordon W. **Smith**	RAF No. 176513	RAF	**RH753**	A&AEE	†
	A passenger, Mr D.E. Purse photographer was also killed in the crash.					

Built as TF.1s, +Met.3, #Delivered as T.4s

Serial	TOC	Operational Units	Cv T.4 (del.)	Cv T.5 (del.)
RH742*	15.01.46	-	-	-
RH743*	16.01.46	-	-	-
RH744*	01.02.46	-	-	-
RH745*	17.08.46	-	-	-
RH746*	16.03.46	-	-	-
RH747*	16.03.46	-	-	-
RH748*	16.03.46	-	-	-
RH749*	17.08.46	-	-	-
RH750*	17.08.46	-	-	-
RH751*	30.01.48	-	-	-
RH752*	17.08.46	-	-	-
RH753*	27.09.46	-	-	-
RH754*	27.09.46	-	-	-
RH755*	30.12.47	Cv B.1 (16.09.49), **45** *(G)*, **84** *(E)*	-	-
RH756	30.06.49	**45, 84**	-	-

Brigand RH757 was stored at 19 MU for almost a year and a half before it returned to Bristol to be converted to a T.4. Its conversion to a T.5 was undertaken four years later. It is seen in T.5 configuration during its time with 238 OCU. The T.5 had a slightly longer nose compared to the T.4.

Serial	TOC	Operational Units	Cv T.4 (del.)	Cv T.5 (del.)
RH757	21.10.49	-	24.08.51	25.11.55
RH758	30.09.49	-	24.10.51	03.12.54
RH759	08.03.49	-	-	-
RH760	20.05.49	-	06.09.51	-
RH761	06.08.48	**84**	-	-
RH762	30.09.49	-	15.11.51	-
RH763	02.01.47	Cv Met.3 (del. 24.02.48)	-	-
RH764	28.04.49	**8** *(B)*	-	-
RH765	15.11.49	-	08.08.51	09.03.55
RH766	30.12.49	-	02.07.51	-
RH767	30.12.49	-	08.08.51	-
RH768	23.09.49	-	15.04.51	-
RH769	23.12.49	-	15.04.51	-
RH770	16.12.49	-	-	-
RH771	14.12.49	-	27.09.51	-
RH772	03.04.47	-	-	-
RH773	30.04.47	-	-	-
RH774	23.12.49	-	27.07.51	29.06.54

Above, RH764/B of 8 Sqn undergoing open-air maintenance. It was eventually struck off charge on 25.02.1953.

Left, Brigand RH774/C was initially converted to a T.4, but was never issued to a training unit and was stored before returning to Bristol for T.5 conversion. It served at 238 OCU between August 1954 and March 1958.

Below, a fully loaded RH776/K of 84 Sqn taxiing for the runway for another strike.

RH775	17.08.49	-	15.11.51	-
RH776	19.11.48	**45, 84** *(K)*	-	-
RH777	30.11.48	**8**	-	-
RH792	28.02.49	**84, 8**	-	-
RH793	11.03.49	**8**	-	-
RH794	13.01.49	-	12.10.51	-
RH795	28.02.49	**8**	-	-
RH796*	05.08.47	Cv B.1 (14.09.49), **84**	-	-
RH797	04.03.48	-	13.03.51	17.10.56

Brigand RH797 served briefly at the RAE and was then converted to a T.4 and stored. It later undertook a T.5 conversion to serve as aircraft 'D' at 238 OCU between October 1956 and March 1958.

RH798	29.04.48	-	-	-
RH799	10.08.48	-	02.07.51	-
RH800	03.01.50	-	30.04.51	07.12.55
RH801	11.04.48	-	04.06.51	-

Brigand RH800 was modified to a T.4 in April 1950 and was issued to 228 OCU. It was then converted to T.5 configuration and issued to 238 OCU as aircraft 'R'.

RH802	20.08.48	-	13.03.51	24.01.56
RH803	13.08.48	-	-	
RH804	26.08.48	-	04.07.51	17.12.54

Brigand RH804/S of 238 OCU, seen as a T.5

RH805	26.08.48	-	04.06.51	-
RH806	07.09.48	-	18.05.51	-
RH807	26.08.48	-	21.05.51	-
RH808	04.10.48	-	09.08.51	-
RH809	20.09.48	**84** *(F)*	-	-
RH810	01.09.48	**84** *(C)*	-	-
RH811	03.09.48	**84** *(G)*	-	-
RH812	08.09.48	**84, 8** *(D)*	-	-

Brigand RH812/D of 8 Sqn during a pre-flight before another routine flight. It was struck off charge on 25.02.1953.

RH813	13.09.48	**84** *(H)*	-	22.07.54
RH814	16.09.48	**8**	-	-
RH815	16.09.48	**84** *(E)*	-	-
RH816	10.09.48	**84** *(B)*	-	-
RH817	03.09.48	**84** *(A)*	-	-
RH818	22.09.48	**84** *(B)*, **8**	-	-
RH819	19.11.48	**8**	-	-
RH820	-			
RH821	-			
RH822	19.01.49	**8**	-	-
RH823	19.01.49	**84** *(A, then P)*	-	-
RH824	-			
RH825	19.01.49	**8**	-	-
RH826	19.01.49	**84**	25.07.51	31.08.54

Brigand RH826/Z was not issued before November 1954 when it was converted to a T.5 (from a T.4). It served with 238 OCU until March 1958 when it was stored for the last time. It was sold for scrap the following November.

RH827	24.01.49	**8** *(F)*	-	-
RH828	26.01.49	**84** *(K)*	-	-
RH829	26.01.49	**45** *(M)*	-	23.02.54
RH830	28.01.49	**8** *(C)*	-	-

Brigand RH830/C seen as a derelict after it was withdrawn from use and struck off charge in situ in February 1953.

RH832/F of 238 OCU in T.5 configuration. It initially served with 45 and 84 Squadrons in the Far East.

RH831	25.02.49	**84** *(E)*	-	14.09.54
RH832	28.01.49	**45, 84**	-	01.07.54
RH850	28.01.49	**45** *(U)*	-	-
RH851	04.02.49	**45, 84**	-	-
RH852	07.02.49	**8**	-	-
VS812	*n/k*	**84**	-	-
VS813	02.03.49	**45** *(Q)*	08.05.52	09.09.54
VS814	20.05.49	**8** *(L)*	-	-
VS815	27.06.49	**8**	-	-
VS816	27.06.49	**8** *(A)*	-	-
VS817+	19.11.48	**1301 Flt**	-	-
VS818+	12.10.48	-	-	-
VS819+	26.10.48	-	-	-
VS820+	30.11.48	**1301 Flt** *(B)*	-	-
VS821+	30.11.48	**45, 1301 Flt**	-	-
VS822+	30.11.48	**45, 1301 Flt**	-	-
VS823+	12.01.49	**1301 Flt**	-	-
VS824+	12.01.49	**45, 1301 Flt**	-	-
VS825+	13.01.49	-	-	-
VS826+	03.02.49	-	-	-
VS827+	13.03.49	-	-	-
VS828+	07.02.49	-	-	-
VS829+	11.02.49	-	-	-
VS830+	10.02.49	-	-	-
VS831+	28.03.49	-	-	-
VS832+	18.02.49	-	-	-
VS833	25.03.49	-	23.11.51	27.05.54

Brigand T.5 VS833/H of 238 OCU.

VS834	27.04.49	-	-	-
VS835	04.04.49	**8** *(M)*	-	-
VS836	22.04.49	**8**	-	-
VS837	11.03.49	-	07.12.51	24.08.54

Brigand T.5 VS837/N of 238 OCU.

VS838	28.04.49	**45** *(A)*	-	-
VS839	12.04.49	**8** *(W)*	-	-
VS854	23.05.49	**84** *(G)*	-	-
VS855	05.05.49	**45** *(V)*	10.03.52	14.06.54
VS856	26.05.49	**8**	-	-
VS857	13.05.49	**45** *(K)*	-	-

Brigand VS839/W of No; 8 Sqn taking off.

VS858#	23.06.52	-	-	-
VS859	09.05.49	**45** *(G)*	-	-
VS860	30.06.49	-	-	-
VS861	14.06.49	**84** *(B)*	-	-
VS862	27.06.49	**8** *(M)*	-	-
VS863	12.07.49	**45** *(L)*	-	-
VS864	19.07.49	**45** *(N)*	-	-
VS865	19.07.49	**84, 45** *(R)*	26.06.52	27.10.54
VS866	28.07.49	-	04.02.52	18.05.54
VS867	28.07.49	-	03.01.52	29.10.54
VS868	03.12.49	**45** *(A)*, **84** *(A)*	-	-
VS869	29.12.49	**84**	-	-
WA560	31.01.50	-	23.04.51	-
WA561#	14.02.51	-	14.02.51	23.11.55
WA562#	23.02.51	-	23.02.51	-
WA563#	27.02.51	-	27.02.51	-
WA564#	27.02.51	-	27.02.51	-
WA565#	11.04.51	-	11.04.51	28.05.54
WA566#	30.04.51	-	30.04.51	19.07.54
WA567#	31.05.51	-	31.05.51	-
WA568#	27.06.51	-	27.06.51	-
WA569#	28.09.51	-	28.09.51	-
WB228	12.02.50	**8**	-	-
WB236	27.02.50	**84** *(K)*	-	-

Two 238 OCU Brigand T.5s, WA561/L and, bottom, WA566/B. Both were sent to 19 MU in March 1958 and withdrawn from use the following month. By the end of the autumn, they had all been sold for scrap.

The Bristol Buckmaster

The specification for the Brigand (Type 164 in Bristol terminology) called for a provision to order a dual control variant, named Brigand Mk.II (Type 165). However, Bristol was anxious not to complicate Brigand development with a trainer variant and in August 1943 suggested a dual-control version of its Bristol Buckingham instead. The Buckingham program had been chaotic with many delays and plans to send Buckingham B.1 bombers to the Far East cancelled after 54 airframes had been built from an initial order of 400 (later reduced to 300 then 119 by VJ-Day). To keep the Bristol workforce busy during the interim post-war period while other types were on the table, the remaining aircraft were built as Buckingham C.1s, fast courier transports stripped of all armament and armour, but with extra tankage for better range and accommodation for seven passengers, while the 54 B.1s returned to Bristol for conversion. However, most of the C.1s remained in storage after delivery and were eventually scrapped after very short flying lives. For the few that actually flew, they operated on courier services to Malta and Egypt, but were found to be uneconomical as load carriers.

The Air Staff accepted the idea for a dual control variant of the Buckingham, which would take the name 'Buckmaster' (Type 166). Using the same Buckingham wings, Bristol designed a new fuselage with a wide forward section for side-by-side pilots' stations and a radio operator behind them. All armament, armour and other military equipment was removed. The first prototypes were built from partly completed Buckinghams and received serials **TJ714** and **TJ717**. The first prototype made its maiden flight on 27 October 1944 and an order for 100 was soon placed, followed by an extra ten soon after, so a total of 112, prototypes included, were built with serials **RP122-RP246** (100 drawn from a Buckingham order) and **VA359-VA368**. Deliveries took place between March 1945 and May 1946. The Buckmaster was mainly used to train Brigand pilots at OCUs, but some machines were also issued to operational Brigand squadrons for training and communication duties. By the autumn of 1956 they had all been scrapped after a low service record. During this short career six aircraft were written off following accidents.

Buckingham C.1 KV365 during a pre-flight check. The first C.1 deliveries were made in late January 1945, KV365 being one of the first two. KV365 was sent to ATTDU (Air Transport Tactical Development Unit) in February 1945 to begin C.1 service trials, later joined by KV369. In August, ATTDU became TCDU (Transport Command Development Unit) and both of these aircraft spent time in the Mediterranean on development flying.

Date	Crew	S/N	Origin	Serial	Unit	fate
12.09.46	F/L Reginald R. **Huntley**	RAF No. 145060	RAF	**RP149**	6 (C) OTU	-
	W/C Gordon C.O. **Key**	RAF No. 37815	RAF			-
09.12.47	F/L John E. **Balzagette**	RAF No. 131145	RAF	**VA361**	19 MU	-
	One more unidentified crewman was on board was also safe					
03.11.48	F/L John P. **Wilson**	RAF No. 56589	RAF	**RP145**	228 OCU	-
	rest of the crew or passengers not reported but safe.					
21.11.51	F/O John L. **Fisher**	RAF No. 202360	RAF	**RP231**	HCCS	†
	F/L Henry R. **Nathan**	RAF No. 129627				†
21.04.52	S/L John W. **Stephens**	RAF No. 40028	RAF	**RP209**	8 Sqn	†

Right, the first Buckmaster proto-type TJ714 in October 1944. Below one of the first production Buckmaster, RP132 taken in March 1945

Top, RP185 while serving with 228 OCU which became the main user of the Buckmaster. Middle, Buckmaster T.1 RP198, which served with 45 Sqn as 'OB-Z' at Kuala Lumpur to train Brigand pilots. Bottom, RP236/K, which was used for the same task at 8 Sqn.
(A. Thomas)

Buckmasters were also used for training purposes by 84 Sqn, like RP235 left, while others served in various OCUs in UK, like RP201, which served all of its flying career with 238 OCU, while many others were never issued to any unit, like RP237.
(A. Thomas - RP235)

Two views of Buckmaster RP245/FCV-E of the ECFS (Empire Central Flying School) in 1946.

✝

IN MEMORIAM

Bristol Brigand and Buckmaster

Name	Service No	Rank	Age	Origin	Date	Serial
ARMSTRONG, James Blakclock	RAF No. 4038565	Sgt	21	RAF	03.05.52	RH755
BLAKEY, Paul	RAF No. 3039885	Sig. III	22	RAF	31.07.50	RH815
BOWDEN, Vernon	RAF No. 1654380	Sgt	27	RAF	15.06.51	VS857
COCHRANE, Basil Alexander Dundonald	RAF No. 607110	F/O	22	RAF	03.05.52	RH755
COX, Walter Edward	RAF No. 4117783	F/Sgt	n/k	RAF	23.02.53	RH760
CROCKER, Ronald John	RAF No. 3509882	F/O	n/k	RAF	08.03.56	RH831
CROSS, Peter William	RAF No. 579191	Nav .III	n/k	RAF	30.12.49	VS839
ELLIS, Bruce Augustien	RAF No. 3045992	Sgt	25	RAF	15.02.51	VS859
FISHER, John Leonard	RAF No. 202360	F/O	39	RAF	21.11.51	RP231
FULLAGAR, Keith John	RAF No. 2360054	F/O	22	RAF	01.06.51	VS869
GREGORY, Harry Louis Paul	RAF No. 583395	F/Sgt	28	RAF	01.06.51	VS869
HALL, Kenneth	RAF No. 579330	Sgt	23	RAF	11.01.51	VS838
HANSON, David Walter Hunter	RAF No. 1545694	F/Sgt	33	RAF	08.03.56	RH831
HARBEN, Norman Brian	RAF No. 2238185	F/O	23	RAF	06.07.50	RH850
HARTLEY, Ian John	RAF No. 111978	F/L	31	RAF	19.07.47	RH752
HAYES, Lionel Vincent	RAF No. 1894918	Sig. II	n/k	RAF	30.12.49	VS839
HAYLER, Sydney Vincent	RAF No.579267	Sgt	24	RAF	11.01.51	VS838
KENT, William	RAF No. 1852236	Sgt	25	RAF	15.02.51	VS859
LLOYD, Clifford	RAF No. 578681	Sig. III	24	RAF	06.07.50	RH850
MATTHEWS, Ronald Edward	RAF No. 133231	F/O	n/k	RAF	19.06.51	RH811
MARSHALL, Desmond Charles	RAF No. 55252	F/L	27	RAF	31.07.50	RH815
MASSEY, Bredan	RAF No. 146871	F/L	n/k	RAF	20.12.52	RH823
MORREN, Thomas William George	RAF No. 48008	F/L	31	RAF	19.07.47	RH752
NATHAN, Henry Richard	RAF No. 129627	F/L	n/k	RAF	21.11.51	RP231
PARKER, William Brown	RAF No. 2523032	P/O	n/k	RAF	23.02.53	RH760
POWELL, Edward Clifford	RAF No. 1580783	Sgt	n/k	RAF	20.12.52	RH823
ROBINSON, George Albert	RAF No. 3032204	Sgt	23	RAF	11.01.51	VS838
SCOTT, Desmond Lionel	RAF No. 3036637	F/O	23	RAF	30.12.49	VS839
SHARKEY, Charles	RAF No. 550949	F/Sgt	n/k	RAF	01.06.51	VS869
SMITH, Gordon Wood	RAF No. 176513	F/L	30	RAF	02.07.52	RH753
SMITH, Tom Walter	RAF No. 578704	Nav. II	25	RAF	06.07.50	RH850
STEPHEN, John William	RAF No. 40028	S/L	n/k	RAF	21.04.52	RP209
SYMINGTON, Alan Archibald James	RAF No. 180387	F/L	26	RAF	23.02.53	RH760
WILMOT, David	RAF No. 2479597	P/O	n/k	RAF	23.02.53	RH760
WRIGGLESWORTH, Richard Stanley	RAF No. 167386	F/L	25	RAF	31.07.50	RH815

Total: 35

n/k: not known

Bristol Brigand B. 1 VS816
No. 8 Squadron
Khormaksar (Aden), 1952

Bristol Brigand B. 1 RH829
No. 45 Squadron
Tengah (Singapore), 1950

Bristol Brigand B. 1 RH776
No. 84 Squadron
Tengah (Singapore), 1952

Bristol Brigand B. 1 RH811
No. 84 Squadron
Tengah (Singapore), 1950

Bristol Brigand B. 1 RH823
No. 84 Squadron
Tengah (Singapore), 1951

Side views - no wings

Side views - no wings

Side view - no wings

SQUADRONS! - The series

1 The Supermarine Spitfire Mk VI
2 The Republic Thunderbolt Mk I
3 The Supermarine Spitfire Mk V in the Far East
4 The Boeing Fortress Mk I
5 The Supermarine Spitfire Mk XII
6 The Supermarine Spitfire Mk VII
7 The Supermarine Spitfire F. 21
8 The Handley-Page Halifax Mk I
9 The Forgotten Fighters
10 The NA Mustang IV in Western Europe
11 The NA Mustang IV over the Balkans and Italy
12 The Supermarine Spitfire Mk XVI - The British
13 The Martin Marauder Mk I
14 The Supermarine Spitfire Mk VIII - The British
15 The Gloster Meteor F.I & F.III
16 The NA Mitchell - The Dutch, Poles and French
17 The Curtiss Mohawk
18 The Curtiss Kittyhawk Mk II
19 The Boulton Paul Defiant - day and night fighter
20 The Supermarine Spitfire Mk VIII - The Australians
21 The Boeing Fortress Mk II & Mk III
22 The Douglas Boston and Havoc - The Australians
23 The Republic Thunderbolt Mk II
24 The Douglas Boston and Havoc - Night fighters
25 The Supermarine Spitfire Mk V - The Eagles
26 The Hawker Hurricane - The Canadians
27 The Supermarine Spitfire Mk V - The 'Bombay' squadrons
28 The Consolidated Liberator - The Australians
29 The Supermarine Spitfire Mk XVI - The Dominions
30 The Supermarine Spitfire Mk V - The Belgian and Dutch squadrons
31 The Supermarine Spitfire Mk V - The New Zealanders
32 The Supermarine Spitfire Mk V - The Norwegians
33 The Brewster Buffalo
34 The Supermarine Spitfire Mk II - The Foreign squadrons
35 The Martin Marauder Mk II
36 The Supermarine Spitfire Mk V - The Special Reserve squadrons
37 The Supermarine Spitfire Mk XIV - The Belgian and Dutch squadrons
38 The Supermarine Spitfire Mk II - The Rhodesian, Dominion & Eagle squadrons
39 The Douglas Boston and Havoc - Intruders
40 The North American Mustang Mk III over Italy and the Balkans (Pt-1)
41 The Bristol Brigand
42 The Supermarine Spitfire Mk V - The Australians
43 The Hawker Typhoon - The Rhodesian squadrons
44 The Supermarine Spitfire F.22 & F.24
45 The Supermarine Spitfire Mk IX - The Belgian and Dutch squadrons
46 The North American & CAC Mustang - The RAAF
47 The Westland Whirlwind
48 The Supermarine Spitfire Mk XIV - The British squadrons
49 The Supermarine Spitfire Mk I - The beginning (the Auxiliary squadrons)
50 The Hawker Tempest Mk V - The New Zealanders
51 The Last of the Long-Range Biplane Flying Boats
52 The Supermarine Spitfire Mk IX - The Former Canadian Homefront squadrons
53 The Hawker Hurricane Mk I & Mk II - The Eagle squadrons
54 The Hawker biplane fighters
55 The Supermarine Spitfire Mk IX - The Auxiliary squadrons

SQUADRONS!
No.3
The Supermarine
SPITFIRE Mk. V
in the Far East

USN AIRCRAFT
1922-1962
Vol.7:
Type Designation Letter
'F' (Pt-4)
Phil H. LISTEMANN

RAF, DOMINION & ALLIED SQUADRONS
AT WAR:
STUDY, HISTORY AND STATISTICS
No.137 Squadron
1941 - 1945
COMPILED BY
PHIL H. LISTEMANN
WITH
CHRIS THOMAS

Fighter Leaders
of the RAF, RAAF, RCAF, RNZAF & SAAF in WW2
Volume VII
IR·G
Phil H. Listemann

SQUADRONS!
No.10
The North American
Mustang Mk. IV
in Western Europe

www.RAF-IN-COMBAT.com
- USN Aircraft 1922-1962 -
- Squadrons! -
- RAF, Dominion and Allied squadrons at War -
- Allied Wings -
- Famous squadrons of WW2 -
- Fighter Leaders -

RAF, DOMINION & ALLIED SQUADRON
AT WAR:
STUDY, HISTORY AND STATISTICS

No.131 (County of Kent) Squadron
1941 - 1945

ALLIED WINGS

Famous Commonwealth Squadrons of WW2
No.453 (R.A.A.F.) Squadron
1941-1945
Buffalo, Spitfire

No.19
Electric CANBERRA

SQUADRONS!
No.41
The Bristol
Brigand